STARFISH

LIVING ☆ THINGS

STARFISH

Rebecca Stefoff

BENCHMARK BOOKS

MARSHALL CAVENDISH
NEW YORK

Benchmark Books
Marshall Cavendish Corporation
99 White Plains Road
Tarrytown, New York 10591-9001

Illustrations by Jean Cassels

Library of Congress Cataloging-in-Publication Data
Stefoff, Rebecca, 1951-
Starfish / by Rebecca Stefoff.
p.   cm. — (Living things)
Includes bibliographical references and index.
Summary: Text and photographs introduce some of the 3600 kinds of starfish.
ISBN 0-7614-0117-2 (lib. bdg.)
1. Starfishes—Juvenile literature. [1. Starfishes.]
I. Title. II. Series: Stefoff, Rebecca, 1951-   Living things.
QL384.A8S84   1997   593.9'3—dc20   96-2080   CIP   AC

Photo research by Ellen Barrett Dudley

Cover photo: *Animals Animals:* W. Gregory Brown

The photographs in this book are used by permission and through the courtesy of:
Animals, Animals: W. Gregory Brown, 7, 16; E. R. Degginger, 10; Colin Milkins,
17 (left); Z. Leszczynski, 17 (right); Kim Westerkov, 26. *Peter Arnold, Inc.:*
Sea Studios Inc., 6; Bob Evans, 8, 19, 24 (left); Norbert Wu, 11 (top left),
24 (right), 27, 32; Fred Bavendam, 11 (top right), 11 (bottom right),
18 (top right), 22. *Photo Researchers, Inc.:* Calvin Larsen, title page; Gregory
Ochocki, 9; Andrew Martinez, 11 (bottom left), 12, 14-15; Carleton Ray, 13;
Fred Winner/Jacana, 18 (top left); Louisa Preston, 20; Stuart Westmorland, 21;
Michael McCoy, 23; Mark Newman, 25.

Printed in the United States of America

3   5   6   4

To my friend Dominique Rose Taverniti-Walton

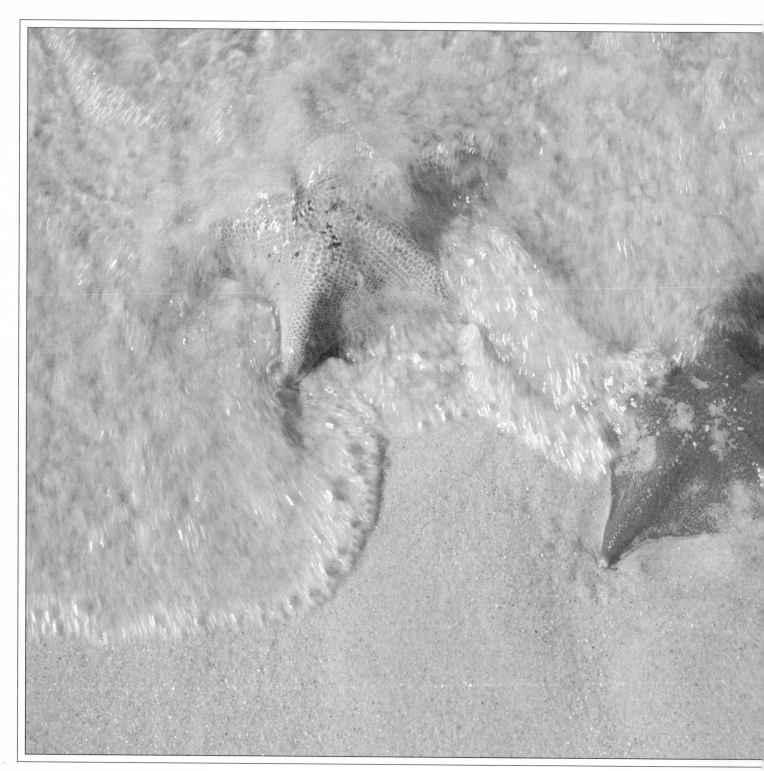

sea stars on a California beach

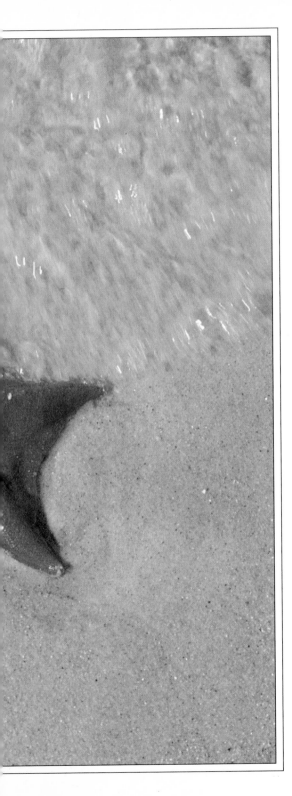

candy cane stars

Imagine that you are walking along an ocean beach. Look! Something bright and colorful is lying on the sand. It looks like a star that has been washed up by the waves. What is it?
You have found a starfish.

sunflower sea star

The starfish is an animal that lives in the ocean, but it is not a fish. Some starfish are called sea stars because they look like stars.

The sea star's arms are called rays. They grow out from the middle of the sea star's body.

Most sea stars have five rays, but some have six, or ten, or even twenty. Try counting the rays on the big sunflower sea star at the top of this page. That's a lot of rays!

small bat star with spiny star

Some starfish have short, stubby rays that hardly stick out at all. Others have long, feathery rays with curly branches.

Can you guess which starfish is called the candy cane star? How about the chocolate chip star?

sea star

candy cane star

pincushion star

chocolate chip star

northern basket star

blood star with sea urchins and sea lilies

There are about thirty-six hundred different kinds of starfish in the world. The smallest starfish are less than an inch across when they are fully grown. The largest ones are more than three feet across (about a meter). Starfish don't have skeletons to hold them up. Their spiny skins give them their shape and protect them.

sea stars near Antarctica

All starfish live in seawater. Most starfish spend their whole lives on the seafloor, but some float slowly through the water. Some starfish like warm water and some like cold water. Scientists have even found sea stars in the waters of Antarctica, the coldest place on earth.

Many kinds of starfish are called brittle stars. The rays of a brittle star are longer and thinner than a sea star's rays.

Brittle stars can walk on the ends of their long rays, like a person walking on stilts. They can also swim, using their rays as paddles. Brittle stars move around much more than sea stars.

northern basket star

Sea stars come in lots of colors. Some sea stars match their backgrounds. This helps them hide from their enemies.

Indo-Pacific sea star

tube feet   *sea star's mouth*

Underneath the sea star's rays are soft tentacles called tube feet. The sea star creeps along on hundreds of these feet.

You won't see a sea star's mouth unless you turn it over. The mouth is on its underside. To eat, the sea star crawls on top of its food.

Some sea stars love to eat clams. But how can a sea star eat a clam that is hiding in its shell?

The sea star wraps its rays around the shell and uses its tube feet to pull the shell apart. Even if it takes an hour or two, the sea star will get that clam. Sometimes a sea star stands on a single ray while its other rays pry the shell open.

Other times the starfish does not have to work so hard for its meal. If it is lucky, it finds a dead crab or a dead fish to eat.

sea star eating a clam

bat stars eating a dead crab

ochre star holding a scallop

bat stars

Sea stars crawl across the seafloor, looking for clams and oysters and other good things to eat. Sometimes they crawl right on top of each other. But they move slowly. It might take a sea star a whole minute just to creep an inch or two.

Sea stars can bend their bodies in all directions. Even a big sea star can squeeze through a tiny hole or crack in a rock.

ochre stars

female sunflower star releasing eggs into the water

new sea star growing from a single ray

Sea stars can do something that almost no other animal can do. If they are broken into pieces, each piece will grow into a whole new sea star. This is one way that sea stars make more sea stars.

They also have babies, just like other animals. The mother sea star lays eggs—from a hundred to a million of them at a time.

bat stars and anemones

bat stars in a tide pool

Sea stars live close to the shore in rocky little ponds called tide pools. Tide pools are busy, crowded places. Sea stars share their homes with other creatures such as spiny sea urchins, mussels, and crabs.

Twice each day, the sea drains away from the shore for a few hours. This is called low tide.

At low tide the tide pools lose most of their water. This doesn't bother the sea stars, though. They can live in the air all day if they stay wet.

sea stars at low tide

firebrick stars with sea urchins and blue maomaos in New Zealand

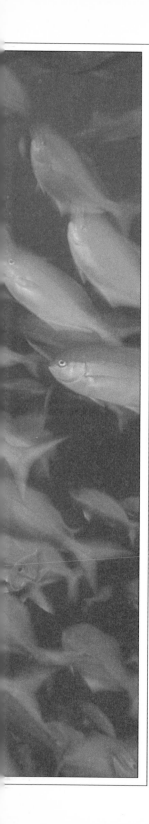

bat stars

Starfish belong to the sea, but they live close to the land, where we can see them. Washed up on a beach or lying in a tide pool, starfish remind us of the magic and mystery of life under the waves.

A QUICK LOOK AT THE STARFISH

Starfish belong to a group of animals called echinoderms (eh KEE noh derms). Other kinds of echinoderms are sea urchins, sea cucumbers, sea lilies, and sand dollars. All echinoderms live in the ocean and have tube feet like those of the starfish.

Here are six kinds of starfish, along with their scientific names in Latin and a few key facts.

BAT STAR

Patiria miniata

(pat EAR ee ah minn ee AHT ah)

Most common sea star between Alaska and Mexico. Measures about 8 inches across (20 cm). Usually has five short arms, but may have any number between four and nine. Generally reddish-orange.

OCHRE SEA STAR

Pisaster ochraceus

(pehs AHST er oke RAH see us)

One of the most common large sea stars on the Pacific Coast from Alaska to Mexico. May be 20 inches across (50 cm). Can be yellow, brown, orange, red, or purple.

CUSHION STAR

Oreaster reticulatus
(or ee AHST er reh tick you LATE us)
Largest sea star on the Atlantic Coast.
Grows up to 20 inches across (50 cm).
Lives in coral or on sandy or weedy
seafloors from North Carolina to
Brazil.

DWARF BRITTLE STAR

Axiognathus squamatus
(aks yo NAY thus skwa MAY tus)
Central body is less than half an inch
across (1 cm). Each of the five arms is
one to one-and-one-half inches long
(up to 4 cm). Lives in tide pools or in
shallow coastal waters from the Arctic
Ocean south to Florida and California.

SMOOTH SUN STAR

Soleaster endeca
(soh lee AH ster en DEH kah)
Usually has seven to fourteen arms
and is purple, pink, red, or orange.
Lives in cold water from Massachusetts
and Puget Sound north to the Arctic
Ocean. Measures about 16 inches
across (40 cm).

29

NORTHERN BASKET STAR

Gorgonocephalus arcticus

(gor gonn uh SEF uh luss ARK tick us)
Central body is about 4 inches across (10 cm). Flexible arms can grow up to 14 inches long (35 cm). Lives on rocky seafloor from the Arctic Ocean as far south as Massachusetts.

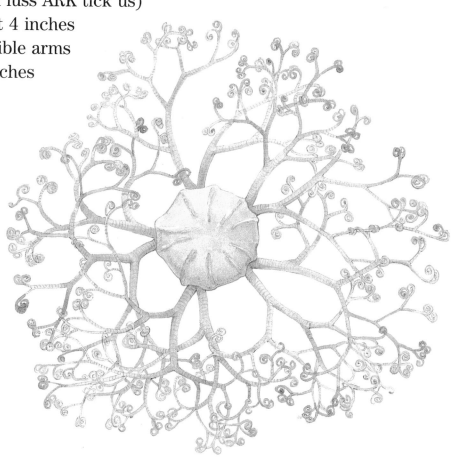

Taking Care of the Starfish

Like all plants and animals that live in the ocean, starfish need clean water, free of pollution. They also need undisturbed areas along the coasts where they can live. By working to keep our oceans clean and to preserve beaches and coastlines, we can make sure that starfish will be around for a long time.

Find Out More

McClung, Robert. *Sea Star.* New York: Morrow, 1975.

Zim, Spencer. *Sea Stars and Their Kin.* New York: Morrow, 1976.

Index

Antarctica 13

birth 23

brittle star 14

crawling 17, 20

eating 17, 18, 20

hiding 16

ray 8, 17, 18

tentacle 17

tide 24

tide pool 24, 27

tube feet 17, 18

Rebecca Stefoff has published many books for young readers. Science and environmental issues are among her favorite subjects. She lives in Oregon and enjoys observing the natural world while hiking, camping, and scuba diving.

candy cane star